THE BEGINNER'S GUIDE TO RAISING CHICKENS

INTRODUCTION

If you are thinking about diving into the world of backyard chicken keeping and care about the quality of life of their chickens, then this is your authoritative guide to coops, nesting boxes, runs, feed, and natural health care for optimal health with time-tested remedies, free of chemicals or antibiotics.

And that means bringing back our tradition: raising chickens! Backyard chickens provide delicious, fresh eggs right from the coop and aren't difficult to raise. Now more than ever, people are looking for sources of convenient, readily available, healthy sources of food for their family.

While raising chickens comes with a few more challenges than a typical pet. However, chickens are smart, social and remarkable animals that make it all worth it. Planning to keeping a few chickens in the back yard really is quite straight forward; however there are some things to consider in order to get the right sort of birds for your situation and to keep them in the best possible health to get the most enjoyment out of keeping them.

Before getting started, check if there's any restriction or law against raising chickens in your neighborhood. Once you've confirmed chickens are welcome in your 'hood and learned about daily care requirements, the next thing you'll need to do is build a coop. The coop keeps your hens safe from weather, predators and pests. Cost for a coop ranges from about $200 for a DIY coop to up to $1,000 or more for a store-bought or custom coop with landscaping.

A typical chicken coop can be made with basic materials like wood, metal mesh, and hardware like hinges and latches. The approximate cost to build a coop yourself would be around $200. For a pre-built coop, there are plenty of options available for purchase both from online and hardware stores in your location.

This book covered lots of area on how to ensure your chickens are safe from predators like hawks, raccoons, rats and dogs, and what safety measures you might need to add like door locks, buried mesh or chicken wire to stop predators from digging their way into the coop.

You'll also need to get bedding, a water dispenser and a water heater to prevent freezing in the winter (depending where you live).

In this book, we will provide you with a guide for beginning backyard farming, covering how to raise chickens from the time they hatch – whether they're feathered, egg-laying friends or raised for meat. How to raise chickens for meat varies slightly from how you raise them to lay hard-shelled, rich eggs. Details like the temperature matter (regarding how to raise chickens in winter), as do the instructions on how to clean a chicken coop! Luckily, we are here to guide you through those details and more as you venture into the world of backyard farming. But before proceeding, let's check out the Cons and Pros of raising chickens.

Pros of Having Chickens in Your Backyard

1. Education: Having backyard chickens allows you to bring your family closer to the process of growing and producing their own food. Sure, you can get through a backyard vegetable garden, but chickens allow your children to see up close and personal the intricacies of food production. And since backyard chickens really become pets, children learn the joys of caring for another being and depending on the age, can provide a large chunk of the support for the hens including daily feedings, collecting eggs, cleaning out the hen house and chicken wrangler.

2. Quality eggs: The eggs that come from your own flock of chickens are truly magical! The first time my girls laid an egg, I was filled with excitement. Very proud of the girls and their achievement and feeling more confident in my chicken raising skills. Eggs from your chickens are going to be more nutritious than a regular grocery store egg, just because of what you are allowing the chickens to eat. You will feed them good quality feed, and supplement with tasty table scraps. Plus, you will have them roam the yard from time to time, eating bugs, grubs, weeds and lots of other tasty treats that are full of nutrients and help provide a wide-ranging balanced diet. The eggs will have less cholesterol, less saturated fat and more omega-3 fatty acids than commercially produced eggs.

3. Compost and garden extras: I may gripe and complain that the chickens do not pull their own weight around the yard, especially when they are molting and not laying, but the manure coming out of the hen house is precious to the urban gardener. You cannot pay for a compost additive as rich as chicken manure! Chicken manure, once composted properly, adds nitrogen, phosphorus and potassium to your garden, better than cow or horse manure. Straight out of the hen house or chicken run, the manure is too "hot" for your vegetable garden and flowerbeds.

I clean my hen house out once a month or so, and dump all the material, manure, shavings, and dry leaves, into my compost box and toss it with the existing compost.

4. Unique pets with personality: The best part about having backyard chickens is the immediate access to pets with unique and quirky personalities. When we first embarked upon our journey as chicken keepers, I was rather sanguine about what would happen when the hens stopped laying eggs (typically they lay 2-3 years). We planned to just "re-home" the chicken and replace with another. After two years, I am not sure I can say the same thing! The hens have become part of our world and their funny antics provide humor and light in our daily lives.

Cons of Having Chickens in Your Backyard

1. Cost: Chicks are so cute when they come home with you. Bubbly little balls of fluff, they just scream to be held and cuddled. However, they don't reach egg-laying maturity until about 6 months of age, which means you need to feed, water and house the little poop machines until they start contributing to the household bottom line.

If you are trying to go organic with your chickens, you can certainly feed them the leftover food scraps from your dining table (assuming you eat a balanced diet of vegetables, fruits and meats), but you will also need to purchase feed, starting with organic chick starter and crumbles and moving to layer pellets. These feeds are high in protein, which the chickens need to keep their feathers healthy and lay good eggs. And this feed costs money, organic or conventional, about $25-30 a month depending on how many chickens you keep.

2. Noise: Oh, wow, can my girls be noisy! And at all times during the day. Astrid, the head hen of the house, has decided she must also take on the role of the rooster, absent in our flock. At 7:30am, or 12:23pm, or 3:33pm, she is known to let rip with a very loud and repetitive "Cock-a-Doodle-Do," which to the uninitiated, sounds exactly like a rooster. I fiddle with the timer on the automatic door to keep them inside until a reasonable time, which sometimes delays her exuberant outbursts, but never for long.

Every time they lay an egg, chickens sing a song, and a couple of the girls are so proud about their achievement that they use their very loudest, outdoor voices. Sometimes, when they are feeling frisky, one chicken will goose the other, and that sends up squawks. No neighbors have complained, yet, but I do make sure to take eggs around to our closest neighbors just as a precaution.

3. Poop: I touched on this above, but the poop is a big deal. You will need to be comfortable with the amount and odor of chicken poop. When they are little and living in the house or garage until old enough to go out to their coop, you will be amazed that such little things can produce so much poop. When they move to their hen house, you will now need to set aside time in your schedule to clean the house often, unless you like the smell of barn in your backyard. And if you let them out to roam around the yard? Be prepared to find their poop everywhere: in the lawn, on the porch, on your favorite loveseat pillow, etc.

4. Lifespan: The biggest con of raising chickens, and the one I start to worry about as we enter year 3 with the girls, is that they only reliably lay for 2-3 years, and then they become garden ornaments for the next 10. By the time they stop laying, you will be so enamored of their presence in your garden that you cannot imagine getting rid of them, whether that is sending them to a "farm" or otherwise relocating. But then you still have to maintain their quality of life in your backyard, and plus you are now back to buying organic, pasture-raised eggs, which helps increase your monthly food costs.

CHAPTER 1- PREPARATION

Chickens are funny, inquisitive, active beings that will provide not only a complete protein food source for you in the form of fresh eggs day in and day out, but also hours of entertainment and relaxation for the entire family - as well as teach children about responsibility and where their food comes from.

Chickens are small and therefore easier and less expensive to take care of than larger livestock - and also allowed in many more urban/suburban areas than say a cow or goat. In preparation to raising chickens, there are certain questions you should answer before raising chickens, such as; But before you dive into the popular pastime of raising backyard chickens, here are a few things you'll want to consider.

The Number of Chickens to Start With

You need to figure out how many chicken you actually "need". A chicken lays an egg almost every day. Not every day, but the good layers come close. So divide that by the number of eggs your family eats in a week to figure out how many chickens you'll need.

The Breed I want

In preparation to raising chickens, you'll need to figure out which breeds you might be interested in. Different breeds of chickens have different characteristics. Some are bred for production and lay lots of eggs, others lay pretty colored eggs, some chickens are good for dual purposes (meaning they lay eggs, but also would make a nice meal!), and others are bred for a calm temperament (these make good choices for families with kids).

Generally any chicken will do okay in a moderate climate, and chickens are generally better in cool climates than warm, but unless you live in an extreme climate, just about any breed will do just fine with the proper shelter.

Should I Start with Baby Chicks?

I always recommend starting out with baby chicks. Not only are they adorable, but you'll end up with a much friendlier and healthier flock if you get them when they're just days old and know what they're eating and how they're being raised right from the start.

Most hatcheries and breeders offer "sexed" chicks, meaning you can order just females, but occasionally you might end up with a little rooster by accident, so just be aware of that if you live in an area where roosters aren't allowed. But for whatever reason, sometimes starting with chicks isn't possible or practical, so know that you can also get started pullets (which means chicks that are maybe 8 or 9 weeks old).

One benefit of getting pullets is that you can be pretty sure you're getting the sex you want, because it's more obvious at that age. You also avoid the whole brooder or "nursery" in the house, since they can go outside into your coop right away.

Another option is POL hens (which means "point of lay", meaning they're about 18 weeks old and almost ready to start laying). Or of course you can take your chances and rescue hens or buy them at swaps or poultry shows as adults. I highly caution anyone doing this because the chance of ending up with a sick bird are very real.

Hatching fertile eggs is yet another option, but I recommend waiting on that until you have a few years of chicken keeping under your belt! It's a bit more involved and honestly can be a bit stressful, but a wonderful experience if you do ever have the chance. Especially under a broody hen!

Where Do Chickens Live?

Your chickens are going to need a place outside to live once they're full grown, or if you started with chickens, once they're able to be outside without supplemental heat at around 10-12 weeks old.

A chickens' home is called a coop or a hen house. You can purchase one pre-built, buy a coop kit, convert a shed or playhouse, or build your own coop from scratch using plans.

Chickens should be locked up at dusk each evening and not let out again until sunrise each morning. Most predators are out during dusk and dawn hours, so erring a bit on the side of caution is a good idea. More details on chicken coop in later chapter.

Where Will my Chickens Sleep?

You'll need roosting bars in the coop for your chickens to sleep on. Wood works best - plastic can be slippery and metal will get too cold in the winter.

A thick branch works well or a 2x4 board with the wide side facing up. Roosts should start about 18" off the ground or so, and be laddered or staggered, so each hen can choose where she wants to sleep. You'll notice that your hens higher in the pecking order (yes, that really is a "thing") will roost up higher.

You'll need something on the floor of the coop to provide a nice soft landing pad when the chickens hop off the roosts, and to absorb some of the manure. I use straw and love it for it's warmth in the winter for my chickens, plus it composts really well in the garden. But large pine shavings is another alternative.

You want to avoid using sawdust which is too dusty or cedar shavings which are thought to cause respiratory issues in poultry. Sprinkling a drying agent on the coop floor will help to control ammonia fumes that come from the manure, as well as kill any mites or lice before they become an issue for your chickens. Diatomaceous earth is my choice - and this one with added essential oils smells absolutely heavenly!

Cleaning the coop on a regular basis is important for optimal flock health. Bleach is a bad choice because if it mixes with the ammonia in the chicken manure, it can create toxic fumes. Instead, white vinegar is a better cleaning choice and adding some citrus oils and other aromatics makes a wonderful smelling all natural coop cleaner.

Bedding needs to be removed and replaced any time you smell ammonia or it becomes wet and packed, and your coop needs good year-round ventilation up high near the eaves for adequate air flow. In the warm months, a thin layer of bedding is fine, but when it's cold, your chickens will appreciate a bit thicker layer of bedding. In extremely cold climates using the deep litter method is an easy way to create some natural heat in your coop.

Adult, healthy chickens don't need heat in their coop. Definitely not if you live somewhere it doesn't even get that cold. Coop fires kill countless chickens and barns and even homes have been burnt down by heat lamps. Dry bedding, chickens and heat lamps are a bad combination, so resist the temptation to heat your coop. Chickens don't need heat.

If you do live in a colder climate, then a coop just big enough for your flock is recommended to give the chickens the best chance of keeping it warm with their body heat. Feed and water should always be outside, not inside the coop. It just adds moisture to the air and attracts flies and rodents.

Where Will My Chickens Lay their Eggs?

Chickens like to lay their eggs in a nice, quiet, dark, secluded place. Nesting boxes can be made from wood, or you can re-purpose things like 5 gallon buckets or even kitty litter trays. You want the boxes to be about 12" square to allow space for just one chicken at a time.

Chickens naturally all want to lay in the same box - usually at the same time - so while the rule of thumb is one box for every 2-3 hens, you can likely get away with just a few boxes even for larger flocks.

Soft bedding in the boxes is important so eggs don't break. You can line the floor of the boxes with an old yoga mat or piece of rubber, and then straw or shavings on top of that works well.

Sprinkling fresh or dried herbs in the boxes can help repel insects and keep your coop smelling fresh. I grow all kinds of herbs such as mint, rosemary, lavender and calendula that I love adding to my nesting boxes during the growing season. Adding curtains to the front of your nesting boxes not only looks pretty, but can encourage broody hens (that is, chickens who want to sit on eggs to hatch them), discourage egg eating and encourage laying in general.

It's always best to collect eggs several times a day. This can prevent accidental breakage, frozen eggs in the winter and keep eggs cleaner. Chickens naturally seek high ground to sleep to be safer from predators, so you'll want to be sure that your nesting boxes are lower than your roosting bars.

Floor level is fine for the nesting boxes, or they can be raised a bit off the floor. If they're any higher than about 18" from the ground, you might need a ladder to help your chickens up into them. Allow for at least 8 inches of roosting bar for each hen. More space is better so they can spread out in the warmer months and stay cool, and they'll snuggle close during the winter months.

The Chicken Yard

Chickens are exceptionally vulnerable to predators and no matter whether you live in an urban, suburban or rural area, there are things that want to eat your chickens. So you'll need to build a yard, or "run" for your chickens to spend their days in when you aren't home to watch them.

Even if you have a fenced in yard, a completely enclosed run is safer because there are aerial threats to chickens like hawks, owls and eagles. And if something can fly into your run, then fox and raccoon can climb over the top to gain entrance as well.

Unlike a coop where bigger isn't always better, when it comes to the chicken run, bigger is always better. Build the largest pen you can for your chickens, but it should never be smaller than a space that allows for ten square feet per chicken. But that's a bare minimum - more is better.

Chickens that don't have enough space can pick on each other and star to get aggressive and bored, leading to feather loss, egg eating and a host of other problems. Although you'll likely have grass in your chicken run for a hot minute before adding your chickens, they'll scratch that down to dirt in the blink of an eye and that's okay. Chickens love to scratch in the dirt for worms, bugs and seeds. Dirt is fine. No need to add anything or even clean out the run. Sunshine and rain should keep your run fairly clean and dry.

Letting your chickens out for "supervised" free range time in the yard is always much appreciated by them. And as long as you stay outside with them, you mitigate the chances of loss from a predator. If you let your chickens out in the late afternoon, they'll automatically return to the coop and put themselves to bed at dusk, making rounding them up so much easier.

But keeping your chickens safe inside their run when you're indoors or no one at home is critical, and be sure to cover your run with some type of fencing to prevent aerial predators and also bury the fencing into the ground to prevent ground predators from digging their way in from underneath.

And it helps to have a small area covered with a solid roof where you can set up your chickens' feed and water and a dust bath area.

WHY RAISE CHICKENS

There are many benefits to owning and raising backyard chickens. Not only can you gather eggs in the comfort and convenience of your own backyard, but you'll benefit from saving a significant amount of money in the long-term. Rather than spending money on eggs and poultry at the grocery store, you can have a steady supply right outside of your own home when raising chickens for eggs.

If you're new to the concept of raising your own chickens, the idea of owning and maintaining a chicken coop may seem a little daunting — and messy. While raising your own chickens certainly doesn't sound like the cleanest activity in the world, the benefits you can reap from properly raising chickens and maintaining a coop outweigh the challenges.

What You Should Know Before Raising Chicken

Check the Regulations: There are rules and regulations guiding every person who is interested in raising backyard chicken. Those laws depend on the person's location or country of residence. You'll clearly need to check with your town or municipality to be sure you're allow chickens where you live. For instance, In Uk there are no national rules or regulations that stop one from keeping small numbers (less than 50) chickens however there are some other regulations to check out.

Like, **DEFRA**, you are allowed to keep up to 50 chickens on your land without registering with DEFRA. However, after the avian influenza outbreaks, a poultry register was set up in 2005 and you are required to register if you keep more than 50 poultry on the premises – so you need to take into consideration any other poultry you have.

Therefore, before setting up a place to raise the chicken ensure you visit the regulation office in your location to get first hand information on the rules and regulations when it comes to raising Chickens. Like some certain properties also prevent people from keeping livestock, with your visitation you'll get to know if you're qualified to raise Chickens.

Although not a legal requirement, it's also a good idea to let your neighbours know if you are intending to keep chickens in the garden to address any fears about noise, vermin, flies or smells.

Enough Time: Do you have the time to look after the chickens? This question is very necessary and you need to answer it in honesty even though chickens are less demanding than some animals, they still need care and will take up your time. As a minimum they must be checked at least once a day, fed, watered and secured at night. Their coop will need regular cleaning too. A variety of other tasks are also likely to require your attention throughout the year.

We discuss more on it when we get to our daily routine task page. You'll see what is involved, and whether this is going to fit comfortably into your schedule.

Expenditure: This involves the cost of raising chickens, starting from setting up their shelter, care, pest prevention and many others. For instance, a solid, weatherproof chicken-house with adequate perches and nest-boxes is essential. Chicken runs must be well-constructed and secure. This initial set-up is the most expensive part of chicken-keeping, but your chickens will be depending on you to provide them with a safe and healthy environment.

A feeder, drinker, vermin-proof storage bin and cleaning-out tools will also be required. The basic running costs include feed and bedding, plus medications such as wormers and mite treatments. You will probably want to supply some supplements and treats too.

As you can see, it's unlikely that chickens will pay for their upkeep in eggs (especially in the short term). It's better to enjoy your chickens as an absorbing hobby – with the bonus of the best eggs you've ever tasted!

Garden Space: Can you possibly spare enough room in the garden to keep chickens properly? Chickens don't necessarily need vast amounts of space, although they will enjoy as much as you can provide. If they are to be kept mainly confined in a run, be realistic about numbers and the area available – allow as much space per bird as possible. Even a small garden can often accommodate a few chickens, but choose your breeds carefully and be prepared to do some extra jobs to keep them happy and healthy.

Priority: What do I expect from my chickens? You really need to know what you want from your chicken. Although the obvious answer to this is eggs, output varies greatly between different breeds, so if eggs are your priority choose one of the hybrid or pure-breed layers. However, chickens come in a variety of shapes, sizes and personalities and there is something for everyone.

Some breeds make lovely pets, some are especially suitable for small children and some can look spectacular free-ranging amongst the flowers. There are chickens that will easily go broody, meaning they stop laying eggs but will hatch and raise chicks for you. There are even chickens that can be eaten. Some breeds will do a little of everything, or you can select one that particularly suits your purpose. There's plenty of choice, just know what you want or your top priority.

Predators: If you have foxes around, free-ranging your chickens won't be an option unless you use electric poultry netting. A nearby badger sett will mean extra vigilance in closing up the chickens at night, plus a really robust house and run. Waterways are often home to destructive mink. Domestic pets, either your own or the neighbours' may also show an unhealthy interest in your chickens. Cats don't usually pose a problem, but dogs can sometimes cause as much destruction as foxes.

Cockerel: Hens will lay eggs without a male being present so it's not necessary to keep a cockerel unless you want fertile eggs (which can be purchased if you fancy hatching a few chicks). All cockerels crow, which may cause problems if you have neighbours and it's not advisable to keep more than one because they often fight.

CHAPTER 2 – SETTING UP THE CHICKEN SHELTER

Building a backyard chicken coop is a commitment of both time and money. Many people don't realize all of the factors that go into building and maintaining a chicken coop before they make the decision, which can lead to problems and frustration.

Just like we said earlier, before setting up a chicken coop, you need to first verify that your local laws allow you to have one in your backyard or home, and if so, what the stipulations are for constructing and maintaining that coop. Once you understand your neighborhood's regulations on chicken coops and maintenance, you need to build your coop according to the number of chickens you're planning to keep, along with other essential factors.

Keep in mind that your coop needs to have the proper structures in place to care for your new chicks, such as ventilation, temperature control, lighting, a predator-proof roof and other necessities. You need to establish a routine for care, as well — who's going to feed and spend time with the chicks as they grow? What happens when you leave town? You'll need a plan of action for regular scenarios.

How To Properly Shelter Chickens

If you live in a volatile climate, it's extremely important to properly shelter your backyard chickens at all times. This prevents them from suffering from harsh climate changes and storms, but it also protects them from predators, harmful insects, and the possibility of escaping. All too often, inexperienced chicken coop owners find out the hard way how improper shelter can be detrimental to chickens and their eggs.

Location & Light

Chickens need a mixture of sun and shade and shouldn't be exposed to excess rain or snow, just like us! We suggest your coop be built near the base of a tree on your property where there will be both sun and shade. UV rays help get rid of mold, ammonia and bacteria. Chickens need light to lay eggs, so when the fall rolls around, many farmers will hook up an artificial source of warm light to extend the laying season and increase egg production.

These lamps should be far away from feathers and bedding, never over 40 watts, and should only be introduced to birds that are 20 weeks or older. You can gradually increase the times the lights are on by 30-60 minutes per week with a goal of 14-16 hours of light per day. It's optimal to add these artificial light hours to the early morning, so the light doesn't automatically shut off when it's black outside!

Chicks: Brooding & Temperature

You wouldn't let a new puppy have full access to your house when you bring it home, right? The same goes for baby chicks. The "brooding period" (lasting in the ballpark of 3-6 weeks after hatch) is a vital time in the chick's lives, as they are the most fragile and in need of warmth and nourishment during this time. It's important to keep the chicks in a draft-free, warm, confined area so they are closer together than they will be later. Always keep food and clean water nearby. Many backyard farmers will use an entirely different space with heating lamps (such as one section of a garage) during the brooding period to ensure the birds survive their younger weeks. When the chicks begin to grow feathers, it's typically time to give them the space of their coop and run.

The Coop

Your coop should essentially be made up of two areas – the enclosed shelter and the run. The general rule of thumb size-wise is one bird per four square feet of space, with a ten-foot run per bird (or more; 10 chickens = 100 sq. ft for the run). A large run with too-few chickens can result in death by freezing in the winter and a small run with too many birds can result in suffocation in the summer. Make sure your coop is the right size and has proper ventilation for the number of chickens you wish to raise.

The run needs to have some kind of ceiling and be protected from all sides from predators such as raccoons, foxes, and rats. If you have your run fenced in, make sure you use something like a net or mesh to enclose the top. A small, dusty area is also essential – chickens like to bathe in dust (doesn't seem so clean, right?!), which not only keeps them happy, but helps prevents mites. We recommend sprinkling Diatomaceous Earth in your dust bath, because bathing in it significantly reduces the chances of the birds getting lice (the most common issue in chicken coops).

Another vital area is a nesting box per every 4-5 hens. These boxes – meant for laying eggs – are enclosed on three sides, with the entrance accessible from the coop. A lot of backyard farmers will attach these boxes somewhere higher up and on the outside of the coop's wall to make it easy to collect eggs (eliminating the need to crawl into the coop)! Thick layers of wood shavings work well for the nest boxes and should be kept clean for clean eggs.

Many coops will have something that allows the birds to perch. Make sure their nesting boxes, food, and water supplies are no where near/below the perch (yes, we're talking about avoiding raining chicken poop!).

Cleaning

We recommend using feed bags or newspaper under wood shavings on the floor of your coop! Using hay or straw might chicken coop with chickens and wood shavings result in mold, which can lead to disease. Shavings are also ideal because they're easier to scoop up and replace. Weekly cleanings of this kind are recommended, but a monthly deep clean is needed, too (think disinfectants – wash the floors and perches of any soil).

We recommend (during this monthly cleaning) sprinkling the dust on their shavings – especially in the nesting boxes – to reduce the risk of lice.

CHAPTER 3 - BUILDING A CHICKEN HOUSE AND BEDDINGS

Chicken houses (often called chicken coops) come in a variety of qualities, materials, shapes and sizes and there are many different variants to suit different circumstances.

Plastic Chicken Houses

There are various popular plastic chicken houses you can use to raise your chickens. We have different manufacturers that produce number of different models and accessories. Mostly, the size of run that the birds get is not that big so you need to consider letting your birds out regularly to free range. If this is difficult, you can easily move most of their coops around. The mesh is sturdy on their runs and there is a flap of mesh around the base that stops predators from getting in but remember the ground must be flat so as not to create a weak point.

They can make a range of different coops and associated accessories such as clip on feeders / drinkers that match the colour of their coops. The biggest advantage of their coops is that it can be cleaned out easily and there are fewer cracks and crevices so it's harder for red mite to take up residence as they are washed away easily.

Unless you have a very large run, you can end up running out of grass, especially in the winter but with an average sized lawn, and a movable run such as the runs supplied by the manufacturer, you should be able to provide your hens with fresh grass every week.

Wooden Chicken Coops.

When buying a hen house, always buy one a little bigger than you need. Hen house manufacturers will give you numbers of chickens that can be housed in a coop but you will find the hens usually need a little more space than this. They assume this is roosting space and you have a contented flock that are happy to roost together. Often this isn't the case and you will find some chickens are at the bottom of the pecking order and don't get the opportunity to roost.

For example, all of the hens want to roost on the one top perch or one hen is being pecked so has to roost with a gap between her and the others or the hens need to stay in their house because of snow or you started with 3 chickens but you've been given another 2 by a friend and so on…. it's so addictive keeping chickens you may want to buy a few more. All of these reasons mean you'll wish you had a slightly bigger house.

DIY For Building Chicken Coop

To create a chicken coop, the chicken coop should have:

Floor Space: A minimum of 30 cm x 30cm (90 square cm) per bird floor area. i.e. If you have a coop that is 90cm x 90cm, this could house a maximum of 9 medium chickens. Do not include nest boxes in this measurement. This should be the inside floor area.

Perches: 4 to 5cm wide perches with rounded edges. At least 40cm long per large fowl and 30cm per medium hen (hybrid size) or bantam. Chickens like to sit down when they sleep and a fairly wide perch helps them balance when sleeping like this. They don't take all of this perch space as they often huddle together but you do need the extra space to allow for gaps so birds lower in the pecking order can still roost away from other hens. e.g. in our example above three perches across a 90cm wide coop is suitable for (90cm x 3 perches / 30cm) = 9 medium hens or bantams, 6 large fowl. Some large breeds will not roost very high and can damage their legs or feet when jumping down from high perches so low perches 30 cm from the floor or a series of perches gaining in height like a sloping ladder is normally better for these breeds.

Nest boxes: It should be provided below the height of the perches to ensure birds don't roost in them and soil them. They should contain straw (not hay due to mould spores that can cause problems) or another suitable nesting material. Aim to provide one nest box for every four hens with a minimum of two nest boxes.

Quality of Chicken Coop And Other Factors

The quality of a chicken coop is important. Generally speaking, the more you pay, the better quality you get, especially with wooden hen houses where the wood costs are the main ingredient. Higher quality chicken coops are made of solid, pressure treated 12mm tongue and groove boards that interlock with one another. Remember thin boards can mean weak doors if you are not careful that can be a problem if you have a determined fox.

Fittings should ideally be galvanised to stop them rusting. This is very easy to check, even when buying online – you can often tell, just by looking at a manufacturer's pictures.

Roof

In days gone by, chicken houses were often sold with a felt roof and the main wooden body of the house was treated with Creosote to weatherproof it. Red mite that live in the cracks of houses weren't really a problem, however since Creosote was replaced with "Creosote Substitute" chicken keepers have been finding their coops full of red mites in the summer months.

So what has this got to do with the roof of the chicken house? Well, felt roofs are all very good until you find the red mite have gone underneath the felt where you can't get to them and as a result, you cannot get rid of the red mites without removing the felt and starting again.

Ideally, you should be looking for a corrugated steel or an onduline roof to prevent this problem occurring. This also has the benefit of providing high level ventilation where the roof meets the wall. Some houses use tongue and groove (interlocking or overlapping) wooden roofs which are normally easy to clean with a hosepipe jet or pressure washer if there is a red mite problem.

Draft Free Ventilation

This is very important – Chickens can withstand the cold and are kept in temperatures as low as -20 in countries such as Canada, however, they need a dry, draft free house to sleep in that is well ventilated. Your coop should have some form of ventilation at high level and some sort of inlet at a lower level. They should not be perched next to an opening as it will be too drafty for them.

Chickens droppings release ammonia which needs to be removed from the house by having good ventilation. The heat from the droppings causes this to rise and with a vent at the bottom to bring in fresh air and a vent at the top to allow the ammonia filled air out, all should be fine. Always point ventilation windows away from prevailing winds and close them up if there is wind blowing in through them because on nights like this, there will be sufficient ventilation through the gaps in the wood.

The real test is to put your head into the coop in the morning before letting the chickens out to see if you can smell ammonia. If there is too much ammonia in the air, your hens lungs and eyes can be damaged. Chickens are particularly susceptible to respiratory problems but this can also stress your hens and lower their immune systems… which in turn increases the chances of disease being picked up.

Nest Boxes

If you buy a chicken house then it should come already fitted out with nest boxes. These are usually added onto the side of wooden chicken houses with a lid to the outside so that you can lift it to collect your eggs. Remember that foxes are quite smart and can usually lift these lids so it is always best to have a latch on the lid that can be secured firmly.

Garden sheds or similar can also be adapted to house chickens and nest boxes can be added to the inside of the shed easily as there is usually more room. You can of course build your own nest boxes out of wood (15 inches square is usually a good dimension) and plastic inserts that allow eggs to 'roll away' out of the nest can be purchased too. An alternative solution is to buy some ready-made nest boxes. Some of these like the Chickbox are plastic and make it easy to remove red mite which can be a problem with the cracks around wooden boxes.

The Chickbox has a roll away plastic tray built in which causes the eggs to roll into a safe area which keeps eggs clean and away from other hens feet when they come in afterwards lay. To collect your eggs, you have to lift the landing perch and then lift the little clear plastic lid. The Chickboxes can clip together side by side to form groups of nestboxes if you need more than one.

Perches

Perches should be sturdy and allow a hen to wrap her toes around the edges. The corners should be smooth to help her do this. The most important thing is they should be higher than the nest boxes are to ensure the hens use the perches at night and not the nest boxes. If they use the nest box, it will need cleaning every day – chicken muck where they lay eggs is not good.

Cleaning

After some use, you will need to wash the chicken house out using a detergent like poultry shield. This helps to remove organic matter (or chicken muck) and also helps to keep red mite under control which can be prolific during the warmer summer months (usually between May and October).

Ideally, you want a coop that has easy access for cleaning and has as many removable parts as possible – droppings boards, perches and nest boxes should all ideally be removable so that you can clean your chickens' house out more easily.

Chicken Runs

The Chicken Run is the next most expensive thing you will buy, next to chicken houses and is most likely to be the weakest link as far as predators like foxes are concerned.

In order to come up with a sensible sized run, you will need to ask yourself the following:

- How many chickens will I have? Always assume a couple more because it is a very addictive hobby and you will soon be tempted to add a couple more hens to your flock.
- What space do they need? There are guidlines but legally a battery hen has enough space…. so perhaps you should consider what a fair size run would be for them to move around in, scratch, dust bath, feed and drink and whether there is enough room for them to get away from another hen if pecked.

The run is there to contain your chickens but also to protect them from predators. We have a number of different chicken runs and I have used several designs over the years but every time I visit a friend who has lost chickens to the fox, they say the same things, either "I didn't want to spend…." or "I didn't have the time to…" and "the fox got in through here…"

So lets look at the options, you can pay for a chicken run that will cost you money or you can build a chicken run that will cost you in time but is less money!

Buying a Chicken Run

Small chicken runs can protect birds and you can let them out when it's safe. Most of the chicken runs that you can buy to fit onto a coop (or that are built into a coop) are rather small in my opinion. There is an answer to this though. Use this run for your girls when the weather is really bad or when there is a higher risk of predators but at other times, open the door and let them out!

The down side to this is that they will spoil a small garden over time with their scratching and dust baths, will eat some of your plants and will leave droppings on paths for you to step in! The good news is they get to free range and will be far happier and healthier hens, you can enjoy having them out and can limit their time out a little to allow the garden to recover. You can of course fence chickens into a certain area of the garden which can help if you have plants that you don't want destroying.

An alternative to letting them out of their run is to use a portable run so you can move them around onto fresh grass at regular intervals. I have done this regularly with my young growers but be warned they soon spoil the ground and need moving every few days if the grass is going to have a chance to recover so make sure you get a house and run that's easy to move on your own or with someone.

When buying a run, you will need to look at the quality of the wire – small rectangular or square mesh wire is better because foxes can't get their teeth in to tear at it. Cheap rabbit wire can be quite thin (especially the cheaper, imported versions from Asia) and I have seen this torn open in weak spots, sadly enough for Mr. Fox to get through. If you decide to use rabbit wire then look for galvanised wire type.

Latches or bolts to doors are important as well. Galvanised fittings will last years so it is worth paying for these. Screws need to be stainless steel so they don't rust.

Foxes will dig under a chicken run. If you have problems with foxes during the daytime (or your chickens are not securely locked up in their house at night) then you will need to consider putting your run onto bricks so that Mr. Fox can't dig underneath. You can put wood chips down inside the run so they can be changed regularly.

Building a Chicken Run

If you are going to build a chicken run, you will need to spend less money but more time. You can of course build a small portable run, much like you would buy and the same things apply to this as I've mentioned above but often, people that are building a run go for a fixed run in the corner of the garden.

Rabbit wire is the most economical choice but do be careful with the quality of it. If it isn't particularly thick, a determined fox will be able to tear at it to get in. A double layer around the lower half of the fence is best if the wire quality is poor.

Ensure that weak points such as where wire joins houses is securely stapled. These areas will need checking regularly for signs of wear and tear. If installed correctly, electric fences are very good at keeping foxes out but on occasions, I've seen a run with a fox unable to get out! Sadly the damage has already been done.

Electric fences are not always suitable for every back garden but even in an urban environment where there are people, you can use an electric wire around the top of a fence to stop foxes climbing over.

Chicken wire needs to be burried at least 6 inches with another couple of inches turned outwards but if the soil is loose, you may need to go down 9 inches or more.

A fox can run up a fence (don't think of a fox being like a dog, they can move more like a cat and can jump and climb really-well) so unless your run has a wire roof, you will need to make the fence at least 6ft high and ideally sloping outwards at the top.

Gates should ideally be made from a solid mesh stapled to a sturdy frame. If this is not possible, at least make sure the gate cannot twist, allowing a predator to get through if pushed in the corners. A fox will easily get through a small hole.

Another method of building a large chicken run is to build some 'chicken run panels'. You can cut all of your wood in one go, with many pieces being the same size. Once you have produced enough panels, you can screw them together making a large run that's easy to assemble. Keep the panels off the ground so they don't rot, a brick base on a small strip foundation is perfect but I've seen people use rectangular posts on their side and (better) old railway sleepers buried in the ground.

How to Build a Chicken Run

Building a chicken run is really straight forward if you have some basic DIY skills and follow some of the guidance I have given above.

There are a number of chicken run designs that manufacturers use and a few other 'home made' runs that are successful.

Here, I am going to call the 'chicken run' an enclosure that could be 3 to 4 meters long, usually attached to the coop, rather than being 'around' the coop and is often covered over.

Start by drawing up the run how you see it in your mind. I like to make notes on my drawing as things pop into my head. This can save you significant time later on if you have thought it through before buying and cutting wood.

Draw a 'close up' of how you are going to make the joints of the chicken run, doors, joint wire and so on.

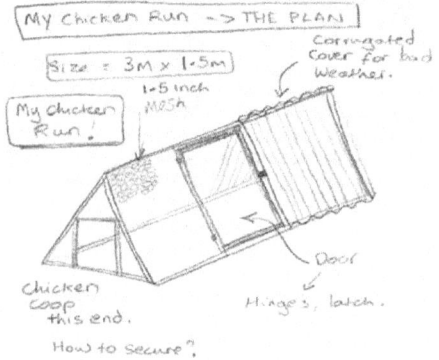

Build a 'cutting list' of pieces you will need to build the chicken run. Turn this into a 'shopping list' by working out how long your wood needs to be and what sort of thickness you will need. Add hinges, latches, screws, nails, poultry netting and staples to this.

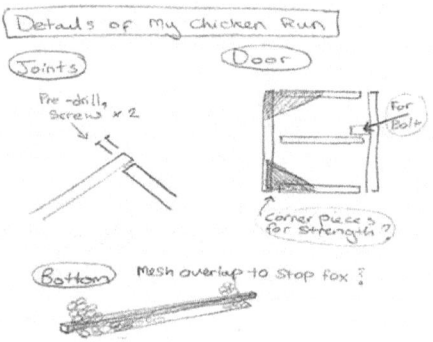

Go and buy your materials, allowing a small amount extra for mistakes!

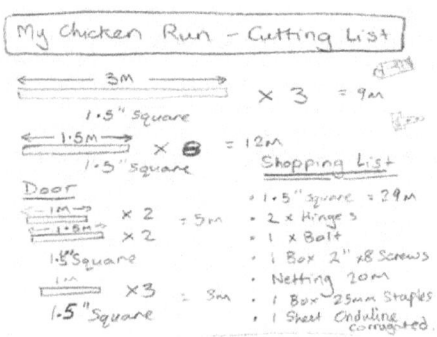

Chicken Fencing

There are a number of options when it comes to chicken fencing. All need to achieve two things though:

- Keep predators out (mainly the Fox in the UK but also Badgers in some areas).
- Keep your chickens where you want them.

The first is of course the highest priority to keep your chickens safe, I am happy to lose the odd plant if an escapee wanders onto the vegetable patch, this is soon forgotten about but discovering birds with their heads removed and bodies half buried is something you don't forget for a long time, if at all.

So what are the options when it comes to fencing chickens? One of the best solutions for me has been an electric fence but this does come at a cost and requires regular maintenance..

Chicken Wire

The good old fashioned way is to use galvanised chicken netting or rabbit wire as it is called in the trade. This needs to be at least 6 foot high and I say this because I have seen a fox leap up and scramble over the top of a 5 foot high chicken run fence when I found him inside one of my runs one morning. Wire needs to be buried in the ground about 8 inches, ideally 12 to be completely safe but if you bend the wire out, you can normally burry it 6 inches with a 6 inch overlap. If you are on sandy soil that is easier to dig, I would consider improving the depth of your chicken fencing.

Another option for securing the base further is to use boards around the base. This helps to keep any substrate inside the run (such as sand, gravel, or wood chips) but also secures the vulnerable bottom edge of the netting that is likely to get tugged and pulled at by a fox or badger and keeps the fencing rigid.

If, like me, you like your chicken run to look attractive, you can of course grow things up the outside of the fencing. I have in the past used a grape vine but the same could be done with many different climbing plants. Try to tie the plant to the wire, rather than threading it through to stop it from damaging the wire when it grows and rubs during the wind.

If chicken fencing is weak, foxes can and will tear at it to try to get in. If the wire isn't taght or if there are weak points, don't wait – fix it.

Chicken Netting

Chicken fencing can be fairly straight forward if you are around during the daytime and don't have a fox problem and would like to keep your chickens in a designated area. This is a great idea as it allows you to easily change the shape and position of the chicken run to provide fresh pasture for them. It keeps your hens where you want them but remember this isn't fox proof or electrified so should only be used to keep chickens in a given area when there isn't a fox problem or when you're around.

It is really good news for gardeners as you don't want the chickens scratching up your beds or eating your new plants! If you turn this idea on its head, you can also use this netting to keep your chickens off your vegetables or garden by fencing the area off to stop them getting in.

CHAPTER 4 - CHOOSING THE RIGHT BREED

If you decided to choose your birds from breeders, ensure the birds you pick are healthy. This is because they can quickly become ill with the stress of the move and pick up any number of diseases. Try to pick the healthiest looking chickens you can. Do not pick birds that are sleepy, wheeze or hold their mouths open (unless it is a hot day), stand fluffed up as if they are cold or birds that have any bubbles or foam in the corner of their eyes. A fit and healthy bird should be active and alert.

Chicken Breeds

Chicken breeds are defined by poultry standards that tell us how a breed should look. A very common misunderstanding with newcomers to the hobby is that all chickens 'are a breed'. Most chickens being sold as egg layers to beginners for backyard flocks are what we call 'Hybrid Chickens'.

Hybrids were originally created in the 1950's as crosses of pure breeds and they were bred specifically to lay a large number of eggs in a year with a good ratio of feed to eggs and would mature and start laying quite quickly. Typically, a hybrid layer will be quite small and lay well.

Most hybrid crosses these days have fancy names like 'Black Rocks', 'Cambridge Blues', 'Amber Stars' and so on but they are not pure breeds. You cannot buy the males (they are sexed as day old chicks and removed) and even if you could get them, they wouldn't breed true. To get more of the same kind of hybrid, you would have to go back to the original parent stock which are often pure breeds or at least, strains originating from pure breeds.

Plymouth Rock

The Plymouth Rock chicken is a wonderful breed of chook for first time keepers and seasoned Chicken Ladies and Lads alike. They are relaxed, resplendent and responsive and make any coop a more loving and fun place to be.

Introduced in the late 1900s, the breed was named after the town of its origin and quickly rose in popularity across America due to their egg-cellent egg laying skills and their laid back look on life. Plymouth Rock hens make great additions to backyard chicken coops and our egg-sperts just love their chilled out vibe and kid-friendly nature.

Araucana

The Araucana originates in South America. Named after the Araucano tribe of Native South Americans. A good looking bird that has an attractive beard and crest. It is a hardy breed that lays a good number of medium sized blue to green coloured egg which makes an attractive addition to any egg box.

They should ideally be kept alone as they can be bullied due to impaired eye sight from their 'head-gear'.

Araucana's have been used to create a number of other blue and green egg layers but also Hybrid chickens that lay these colour eggs will have also come from the Araucana's genes at some point.

Orpington

The cute, courteous and courtly orpington chicken might very well be one of the best mother's in all of the animal kingdom. Created by British poultry breeders at the turn of the 20th century, the orpington chicken was designed to be a hardy breed that can endure England's most bitter winters, whilst still laying at an unstoppable rate.

These heavy-set, fluffy and cuddly ladies will be a figure of grace and dignity in any coop. Orpington chickens may seem homely and commonplace however these powerhouse egg laying wonders will make an eggstraordinary addition to any chicken lovers flock.

Australorp

The Australorp was developed in Australia from imports of Orpingtons. The British continued to develop the Orpington for show making them profusely feathered and it is said that the Australorp was left alone, much more like the original Orpingtons that William Cook had created with better utility (meat and egg laying) qualities.

A good layer that is a calm / docile breed suitable for beginners. Australorps are active foragers and are reasonably hardy. Being a heavy breed, they cannot fly well so can be contained within low fencing. The black Australorp's colouring is beautiful, their backs and wings have a green iridescent sheen.

New Hampshire Red

The New Hampshire chicken breed is a reliable and robust hen that doesn't disappoint when it comes to producing delicious eggs or forming wonderful feathered friendships. These girls are gentle and warm, make egg-cellent mums and are quietly beautiful. Think of the New Hampshire chook as the hen-next-door, an unassuming chicken that is definitely more worthy of your attention than her looks let on.

The breed was developed in the early 1900s by New Hampshire farmers who wanted to improve on the existing Rhode Island Reds and have a chicken breed to call their very own. The farmers focused on breeding hens that were fast growing, early to lay and hardy in the bitterly cold winters of the north-eastern US state.

Croad Langshan

The Croad Langshan chicken arrived in England in 1872 when they were imported by a British Army major called 'Croad'. They are strong, heavy birds and are calm / docile in nature. Croad Langshan's do not fly so can be kept behind low fences although their feathered feet mean they should not be kept in muddy conditions.

You will ideally need a covered run with a dry substrate like hardwood chippings or sand to keep them clean over the winter months. This breed of chicken is a 'dual purpose utility breed', useful for both the table and as an egg layer. The black Croad Langshan is the most popular but white is also available.

Rhode Island Red

Rhode Island Reds are the go-to chicken breed for backyard chook keepers who want a laidback layer to add to their flock. These hens are renowned for their hardiness in any type of environment. Rain or shine, snow or summer sun, the Rhode Island Red is happy-go-clucky in any type of backyard. They are a girl with grit, but don't let that robust demeanour fool you, these ruby red ladies also possess a lot of heart!

They make the perfect companion pet for any Chicken Lady or Lad and a great friend for kids, both big and small. Developed on the poultry farms in Little Compton, Rhode Island in the late 1800s, the Rhode Island Red breed grew in popularity throughout the United States, eventually becoming the state bird of... you guessed it - Rhode Island! A well-deserved honour for such a friendly and easy to care for chook.

Leghorn

Leghorn chickens are adventurous, spirited, friendly and wondrous egg-layers. First developed in Livorno (Italian for "Leghorn") in Tuscany and brought to Britain in the late 1800s, they became a popular purebred chicken in America and later Australia.

The Leghorn chickens' egg laying prowess, savvy attitudes and bold personalities made them the most common purebred fowl in Australia in the early to mid 1900s. We love Leghorn chickens, and not just for their ability to lay generously sized, bright white eggs on a regular basis.

Wyandotte

The silver laced Wyandotte was the first colour variety to be developed in America, being standardised in 1883. It is available in both large and bantam varieties. The Wyandotte is a popular breed that is found all over the World and a multitude of colour varieties have been created, some only relatively recently.

Wyandottes are calm / docile and friendly birds that can become very tame if handled regularly.

They are good egg-layers laying around 200 eggs per year but are prone to broodiness which isn't always desirable as hens will stop laying whilst sitting and their condition deteriorates.

Sussex

Sussex chickens are a brilliant addition to any backyard chicken coop looking for a chook with grace, a friendly nature and a little grit. Their long and distinguished family background and kind and curious nature make Sussex chickens perfect for novice chicken keepers and those wanting a friendly hen to add to their growing backyard menagerie

You'll never be alone with a Sussex chicken, these girls make wonderful companion birds. They enjoy the spoils of being part of their beloved family, foraging alongside you and taking a turn about the garden grounds, but are just as content when mingling with their fellow splendid fowls in the garden, the coop or the chicken run and finding their place in the pecking order of society.

Selecting a Breed

The chick breed and gender you select should consider several variables, including the climate of your home's location and how you'd like your flock to behave. Some breeds do much better in the cold than others, some lay more eggs than others, some are calmer than others. Appearance is a factor, too!

When it comes to the sex of the bird, we highly recommend more hens (female chickens) than roosters (the guys)! Roosters, though protective and often beautiful in appearance, can be jealous to the point of harm. They will often fight over the hens, not to mention they are loud and obviously cannot lay eggs. One rooster in your flock of less than ten birds is a great number.

Alao, there are literally hundreds of different breeds of chicken to choose from and out of these, many have slightly different requirements.

Some breeds of chicken come only as Large Fowl, and others are also available as Bantams which are a smaller version that look the same. The Orpington for example is available in both large and bantam sizes but the Cochin is only available as large fowl.

There are a handful of 'True Bantams' where there is no large fowl equivalent. Examples of these are Dutch Bantams, Japanese Bantams and the popular Pekin Bantam.

Bantams tend to be quite flighty whereas the heavy breeds of large fowl often cannot fly more than a few inches off the ground. Orpingtons for example won't usually roost very high due to their huge size and will usually just huddle on the floor of the coop.

Every breed is slightly different in the amount of eggs they lay. Typically hens that have been bred for exhibition purposes do not lay as well as utility hens. Bantams of course lay smaller eggs which some people say they prefer for taste.

Hybrids

Hybrids are chickens that have been created by crossing pure breeds. They are typically crossed to make good layers, coloured eggs or attractive hens. Some can be very attractive and they are all generally very hardy. Hybrids are produced in larger numbers that pure breeds and most of the crosses used make the males a different colour as day old chicks so that only females can be raised, therefore reducing costs by about half. A typical hybrid hen will cost you around $15 to $30 for a typical pure breed hen.

Hybrids are a good choice if eggs are one of your priorities although if you think you might like to hatch some eggs, remember hybrid hens do not breed true – you would need the original pure breeds to cross again in order to create more of the same thing so whilst you can hatch their eggs, you may want to consider a few pure breeds for this purpose or consider buying in eggs to hatch.

Free Range

You will of course need a chicken coop but also a secure run or area that is predator proof. A question that people always ask is "How big should their run be?" I always say "as big as possible within reason." Even 2 chickens kept in a 2 meter run will soon turn it to mud and get bored (which can introduce vices such as feather pecking and egg eating) but I always believe that it's fine to provide a small run if you can let them out for a few hours each day to free range while you are around. This will give them a chance to forage, supplement their diet and reduce boredom. We will discuss more on chicken run in this book later.

Once chickens have settled into their new house, they will go back to it to roost every night so you can let them out in the late afternoon, knowing they will come back to roost at night keeping everyone happy! Some houses and runs have handles or wheels that make them easy to move onto fresh ground which is not only good to prevent a build up of worm eggs and disease but also provides them with a little fresh grass to graze.

Where to buy Chickens

I have listed these in order of preference – you are more likely to get better quality birds at the top of this list, not necessarily the cheapest price though.

1. Known Breeder: Pure Breeds from a known breeder who has won shows with their birds. These people have spent years on their line of birds, improving them and they are very passionate about the breed and will be able to tell you all about them. They are usually good quality, healthy birds.

2. From a poultry show: There are often sale pens at shows where you can spend time looking at the birds and choosing the best quality birds. You can even ask advice of others around you or from the experienced show staff. If the show organisers are doing their job properly then they will not allow any birds that look sick to be put into the sale pens. Many of the sale pens at shows will have stock from breeders that are showing their birds and will be of reasonable quality.

3. From a private ad or breeder: These people have usually hatched a few birds themselves or hatch a good number of birds to sell. The quality can be variable so you will need to examine the set-up and of course the birds carefully. Private ads can be found on poultry forums in the for sale areas. If the forum is a good one, they will make sure a location is specified in the title of the post.

4. From a Poultry Auction: Some dedicated poultry auctions can sometimes have reasonable quality stock but be warned, some of the more common livestock type auctions can be a great place for people to get rid of their sub-standard or unhealthy birds.

Where ever you end up buying your birds from, if you make sure they are fit and healthy, you generally shouldn't see any problems. If you already have chickens and are adding to your flock then you can be bringing disease in so always remember to quarantine your new birds for at least a week before introducing them to your flock.

5. Hatching your own: Many beginners are starting to hatch their own chickens, especially now that incubator prices have come down and are easier to operate. With sites like eBay advertising hatching eggs, it is often relatively simple finding the breed you want online although hatching eggs that have been through the postal system can be a little hit and miss at times. Check out the egg hatchery chapter to provide you with the step by step guide to hatching your own.

Also, don't forget to take a box! Most breeders ask you to bring your own carriers or suitably sized cardboard boxes to transport your chickens in.

If you're using a cardboard box, it's important to cut some good size slots in the top and the sides to allow sufficient ventilation. Do not put too many chickens into a box. There should be at least a 4 inches of space around each bird so they don't overheat. Make sure they travel on the back seat or in an estate / open boot and keep the temperature in the car cool during the journey. I have heard of people arriving home to find chickens suffering from heat exhaustion in their box and sadly on one occasion I heard of someone who had dead chickens when they opened the box.

Keeping Chickens in the Garden

If you have a 'nice' garden that you don't want spoilt, it's usually a sensible idea to limit their foraging. Chickens scratch at the ground, make dust baths in the dry soil, leave muck wherever they go and destroy tender young plants. If you can plant in pots, this will help and fencing off part of the garden is usually a good choice to keep them out if you have tender or precious plants.

Chickens with feathered feet scratch less and bantams can clear a 6 foot fence if they want to. Heavy breeds of large fowl can be kept out with a knee high fence or box hedge. If you want to stop a bird from flying then you can clip one wing (not both). So you have decided on the breed that's right for you and your circumstances. Next, you will need to think about keeping them secure from predators in a suitable chicken house and chicken run.

CHAPTER 5 – RAISING BABY CHICKS

When you set up a chicken coop, you'll most likely have a tiny flock of baby chicks en route to your home. While these precious little critters are relatively low-maintenance compared to other animals, they require a substantial amount of care and time. Before you get baby chicks, you need to have your coop set up to accommodate them by installing the proper structures, such as heat lamps, nesting areas, ventilation, and other essentials.

Raising baby chicks takes time and patience. In addition to keeping them in a tall brooding box with soft bedding, you need to keep their environment at a consistent 95 degrees Fahrenheit and reduced by five degrees Fahrenheit each week until their environment reaches ambient temperature. Raising baby chicks requires consistent care and attention, but it's also an incredibly rewarding experience!

How to Keep Your Chicks Healthy

In addition to keeping your chicks' environment in optimal condition, feeding your chicks the right nutrients based on their growth stages is extremely important. Depending on your chicks' ages, you should give them different portions and nutrient ratios.

Timing the Arrival of Your Chicks

Baby chicks need to be kept under a heat lamp in the house for the first eight weeks of their life. Until they grow their feathers, they can't keep themselves warm on their own. Chicks grow fast, so time their arrival carefully in order to get them outside as quickly as possible. To do that, count back eight weeks from the time you expect the nighttime temperatures to stay consistently above 55 degrees and schedule that date for your chicks to arrive.

Supplies

Before your chicks arrive, you'll need a brooder for them (a cardboard box or plastic tote works just fine), a heat lamp, a chick-sized waterer and feeder, and chick feed. Until they're eight weeks old, your chicks should eat chick feed, then switch over the starter/grower until they are 18 weeks old, at which point they need layer feed.

Training Your Pets

Dogs are the number one killer of backyard chickens. No one wants to believe their golden retriever could ever harm another animal, but the reality is, if you don't train your dog to behave around your chickens, you might very well lose them to your beloved family pet. So plan on doing some basic training with your dog prior to getting your chicks, including commands such as "drop it," "leave it," "stay," and "sit."

When your chicks arrive, let your dog investigate their brooder and allow supervised time around the chicks. Once the chickens are outside, leash your dog and give stern corrections any time a move is made to lunge at them. Dogs should never be allowed to chase chickens, even in play. Once boundaries are set and respected, your dog should actually become your best predator deterrent and a wonderful guardian of your flock.

CHAPTER 6- HEALTHY FEEDING AND TREATMENT

Now your birds are available. What next? Feeding backyard chickens is the next and very important factor in raising chickens. Chickens' main diet needs to be a balanced poultry feed that's appropriate for their age. Basically there are three stages of growth: chick, grower and layer.

- Chick feed: Hatch to 8 weeks
- Grower feed: 9 weeks - 18 weeks
- Layer feed: 19 weeks+

Chick feed is high protein for the fast-growing chicks and comes in a crumble form that's easy for the little ones to eat. Medicated chick feed is available and offers added protection to your chicks from coccidiosis which can be fatal while their immune systems have yet to fully develop.

The choice to feed medicated feed is a personal one and not necessary. Organic chick feed is also available. Grower feed is a bit lower in protein because the chicks aren't growing quite as fast any longer. Grower feed is available in crumble or pelleted form and both contain exactly the same nutrients, except for the size and shape. Some flocks seem to prefer crumble, others pellet, so you can experiment to see which works best for you.

Layer feed is similar in in protein levels to grower feed, but contains more calcium, which laying hens need to lay eggs with nice hard shells. Layer feed also comes in crumble or pellet, with organic and whole grain formulas also available.

Chickens won't overeat their feed, so you can leave it out for them all the time and let them pick at it when they get hungry. An adult chicken eats about 1/4lb. (approximately 1/2 cup) of feed a day. You can supplement their diet with healthy treats, limiting the treats to about 10% of their diet. Chickens also need two supplements: grit and calcium. These two supplements perform very different specific functions.

Since chickens don't have teeth, they need something to help grind up the food they eat. That's where the grit comes into play. Grit is nothing more than small stones and rocks that the chickens eat and store in their crop or gizzard to help digest what they eat.

Chickens that are allowed to free range at last some of the time will likely pick up enough pebbles as they wander around. Otherwise you'll have to provide commercial grit for them.

Chickens also need supplemental calcium to ensure strong eggshells. Commercial oyster shell is one option; another is crushed eggshells. Which ever you choose to supplement your chickens' diet with, it should always be fed free-choice so each hen can eat as much or as little as she needs. Better layers will need more calcium, young non-layers or older hens and roosters won't need any.

Other natural supplements such as dried herbs, sea kelp, probiotics, brewers yeast and garlic can contribute to your flock's immune, digestive and respiratory health. My line of all natural poultry feed supplements are a great way to be sure your flock is getting all the nutrition they need.

Water For Chickens

Chickens need access to fresh water all day long. It should be cool - chickens don't like to drink warm water. In the summer months, putting out several waterers or tubs of water in the shade is a good idea, especially if you're not home all day.

Adding a Tablespoon of apple cider vinegar to the water a few times a week helps balance the pH, prevent algae from forming in the water and improves digestive health for chickens. A garlic clove crushed and added to the water on occasion will boost your chickens' immune system health. However, let's learn more on their drinking water.

More Details You Need To Know About Water:

Dirty Water or Bacteria Soup?

Water needs to be fresh just like I stated above and if you leave it in the container for a few days at a time, it will start to go stagnant and turn green.

Now I hear you say that chickens can drink out of a muddy puddle and it does them no harm? That water is usually fresh rain water and the mud will certainly not harm them – but water kept in plastic containers that has turned green should be thought of as "bacteria soup" because it's full of bacteria that can harm them.

Green drinking water is a sure way to be asking for trouble with diseases and should be avoided. Changing their water daily or every-other day is easy enough and if you rinse the container out, you can use a small washing up brush around the lip and inside to remove any build-up of anything nasty.

A chicken's body is constantly challenged by bacteria that cause diseases in their environment. Their body will build up an immunity (known as acquired immunity), however giving them large doses of "bacteria soup" will risk them becoming ill so please change water daily or at least every other day.

When you change their water, watch them rush over and take a drink – they do appreciate clean drinking water!

Carrying Chicken Water Containers

Water needs to be kept in the shade during very hot weather: Chickens can handle the cold very well, they fluff up their feathers to trap air which insulates their body, however they can't handle the heat very well. Chickens can't sweat, they can only pant to lose heat through the air they breathe out and drink water to cool themselves down. During very hot weather, it is best to place their (fresh) water in a shaded position.

Water containers left in the sunlight can soon heat up the water inside to a high temperature which means chickens can't lose as much heat by drinking so please, keep their water in the shade during hot weather and if you can, give them some fresh, cool water when it's hot.

Water containers

Water containers for chickens come in a variety of shapes and sizes to suit your needs. Some are galvanised and will last a very long time but the majority are plastic.

Galvanised Containers:

- Last a life time, withstands Knocks
- Withstands frost
- Cannot be used to give Apple Cider Vinegar since the acid corrodes the galvanising
- Doesn't show you how much is left in the container.

Plastic Containers:

- Can be used to give Apple Cider Vinegar in the water
- Shows you how much water is left
- Will only last a couple of years – bases crack, locking bits snap off or handles break, colours fade in the sun.
- Will crack if you drop or knock it when full.

Grit

There are two types of poultry grit available. Flint grit or insoluble grit which is used for grinding down food and Oystershell grit, a source of calcium to help form strong egg shells.

Flint or insoluble grit

Chickens don't have teeth, apparently, they are very rare, so to grind down their food, they use a strong muscular organ called a gizzard. flint grit for chickens

Chickens pick up grit whilst foraging, which is kept for a while in the gizzard to perform this grinding process. If your chickens are kept truly free range then they will find enough of this on their own but these days, few of us have the space or the security from predators to be able to allow them to do this naturally.

Flint (or insoluble) grit is cheap and available from most good pet or farm shops, the container you put it in costs a little more though if it is going to last.

Oystershell or soluble grit

In order to form strong egg shells, chickens require a certain amount of calcium in their diet. Most of an egg shell is made up of calcium. These days, with the research that has been done for formulated feeds (available as layers mash or layers pellets), it isn't so critical to provide oystershell grit because layers feeds contain sufficient calcium, however, it's cheap and it's easy to mix some in with the flint grit that they need above so it's a good idea to provide some, in case they need more calcium.

High production hybrid hens are capable of producing a staggering number of eggs in a year on very little feed (known commercially as the 'conversion ratio') so they are more likely to need the extra calcium to be able to produce the right number of eggs of sufficient quality.

If you can't find Oystershell grit from your local store, baked, crushed egg shells will do the same job – after all, they are mainly made up of calcium. Put them in the oven for 10 minutes to dry them out and crunch them up before mixing them in to your grit hopper.

Grit hoppers

Grit containers come in a variety of shapes and sizes – the priority is really to make sure it doesn't get tipped over or filled up with water.

Specific Feeding Guide For Layer And Broiler

If you've found yourself wondering, the difference between raising chickens for eggs and meat, we've got you covered.

Layer Chicken Feeding Guide

When raising baby chickens who will eventually lay eggs (or pullets, as they're called before they begin laying), it's important to make sure your feed is in crumble form (pellets are difficult for chicks to handle at a young age) and has a higher protein content than the feed you'll switch to after they begin laying eggs.

You'll need an organic Chick Starter/Grower Crumbles, they are a perfect option and should be provided free-choice (meaning the food is always available to the birds). Most have upto 18% protein, and are specially formulated for egg-laying chicks, and are carefully balanced to provide high energy with a good balance of protein, amino acids, vitamins, and minerals. They mostly come as a complete feed, so there's no need to add anything to complete the chicks' diets, but it's fine to supplement oyster shell or calcium chips free-choice from 15 weeks until first eggs. When you see those first eggs, switch your flock to other organic egg layer Pellets or Crumbles (both should also be provided free-choice).

Meat Bird (Broiler) Chicken Feeding Guide

When raising chickens for meat, we recommend the same diet mentioned above of an organic Chick Starter/Grower Crumbles Crumbles, but suggest switching your broiler flock to other organic Broiler/Grower Pellets (free-choice) three weeks after they hatched. Always provide fresh, clean water.

There are many ways to feed your chickens, and we have some really great DIY ideas. Always make sure your waterers (also known as a "drinker") and feeders (also known as a "hopper") are away from any coop perches to prevent soiling. Many feeders are suspended from the coop ceiling, with the feed landing right around the birds' shoulder in height.

Because pecking at each other can result from boredom (or in some cases, a lack of protein in the diet!), providing some kind of activity for the birds to occupy their time with is encouraged. We recommend providing the birds with an organic poultry scratch Grains during the day. They're a nutritious treat for the birds, to be given in addition to their complete feed. The grains encourage healthy eating patterns and give the birds something to do. Another way to entertain them is with pecking stones, which are made of relatively the same ingredients as our scratch grains, but formed into a tough block that the birds can peck at when bored (also called flock blocks, scratch blocks, and/or poultry blocks).

CHAPTER 7 - EGG HATCHERY

Your backyard chickens will lay eggs for 3-4 years and then production starts to drop off. However, a chicken can live for another 6 or more years, so be sure to think about plans beyond the first few years.

When will my Chickens start Laying?

Chickens will start laying eggs somewhere around 5 months old. Switching to layer feed won't make them start laying! Each will start when she's ready. Some of the larger breeds and the colored egg layers can take longer to start laying eggs. While some hens might start laying as young as 16-18 weeks old. Chickens lay an egg about every 26 hours, but no chicken lays every day. They take breaks here and there.

Fresh eggs shouldn't be washed until you're ready to use them. There is an invisible coating on the eggs that protects the egg from air and bacteria entering through the pores in the shell. Washing removes that coating. As long as eggs haven't been washed, they don't need to be refrigerated, but an egg will last seven times longer chilled in the fridge.

Chickens lay well for the first 2-3 years, and then you can expect egg production to drop off about 20% per year until the chicken approaches 5-6 years old and likely will stop laying.

Getting Eggs and Even Meat From Your Chickens

When your chickens start laying eggs, it's important to have a schedule for collecting them. If given 12 to 14 hours of sunlight per day, chickens will typically lay their eggs once or twice — so you need to gather them at least once every 24 hours. Make sure that your coop has enough room for you to enter and collect eggs without disturbing your chickens' environment too much.

Whenever you enter the chicken coop, close the coop door behind you so none of the chickens can escape. You also need to ensure that your coop has sufficient lighting, either from secure windows or overhead electrical light fixtures.

Chickens will typically start laying eggs at around 18 to 20 weeks-old. Most chickens lay their eggs consistently for around three years before egg production slows down. Many chicken owners find that their older hens give them larger eggs, despite the decreased frequency.

Another factor to consider with egg-laying hens is the season. Hens usually stop laying eggs during the winter due to the drop in temperature, but you can work around this issue by installing a heat lamp in your coop for colder months. However, there's nothing wrong with giving your chickens a natural "break" from egg production periodically.

When your backyard flock completely stops producing eggs, you may consider using them for meat. Keep in mind that older chickens tend to have tougher meat, so the ideal time to slaughter a chicken for the tenderest meat is when the chicken is between two and three years old. If you would rather keep your older hens around, though, they tend to provide motherly support for chicks and younger hens entering the roost.

How to Hatch Eggs

Natural Method

If you want eggs to hatch, the best and most natural hatching route is to allow a mother to warm and protect them. Eggs should be kept warm and at a consistent temperature in a secure brooding box with soft bedding. Just make sure you have a brooding hen or two around if you're trying to hatch eggs — they won't hatch if there's no hen to sit on them.

Other Methods for Hatching Eggs;

Hatching eggs can also be very rewarding experience and many beginners are buying incubators since they have become far more affordable over the last few years. Some incubators for small scale have excellent range that can accommodate 20 to 25 chicken eggs, perfect for the beginner to hatch their own eggs.

Before Starting

Before you incubate and hatch chicks, you should remember that you will end up with a ratio of half male and half female chicks. Unless you are hatching an autosexing breed (where markings or colour of the chicks are different colours) or have crossed two birds that give a sex-linked chick (again, different down colour or markings) then you will need to think ahead to when the young growers can be sexed around 8 weeks of age and consider what you will do with the excess of male birds. Sadly, they are very hard to re-home, everyone has the same problem: too many boys.

Choice of incubator

There are essentially two types of incubator –still air and forced air. The big difference between the two is the forced air uses a fan which circulates the air inside. When you measure the temperature, it should be the same throughout. The still air incubator has a temperature gradient inside so the hotter air rises to the top and there can be several degrees difference between top and bottom.

For the average beginner wanting to increase the size of their flock, a forced air incubator is in my opinion the best choice. If you can afford a model that has automatic humidity control then you should have far more success than setting and maintaining the humidity control on a manual unit.

Incubating Chickens Eggs

Chickens eggs have a 21 day incubation period (isn't that amazing? Egg to chick in just 3 weeks) and require a constant temperature of 37.5°C. Eggs will start to produce their own heat in the latter stages of development but the incubator thermostat takes care of this, keeping the temperature the same throughout the incubation period. Humidity should ideally be between 45 and 50%. Eggs need turning regularly by 180 degrees and you will need to do this yourself if the incubator doesn't have an automatic turning mechanism. Expect 50% to 75% of your eggs to hatch, not all eggs will be fertile.

Hatching Eggs

Eggs need to be fertile so a cockerel needs to be running with the hens for a few weeks before eggs are taken for hatching. If you have a cockerel, you can collect your own hatching eggs from your chickens. Try to pick good looking 'egg shaped' eggs, this will help the chicks form and hatch correctly as mother nature intended. Keep nest boxes clean and don't set any soiled eggs. If you don't have a cockerel or would like a different breed, there are many hatching eggs for sale online on sites such as eBay but keep in mind that just about anyone and everyone sells eggs so birds vary in quality between sellers. Hatching eggs travelling through the postal system can be damaged internally and either not develop or die before they hatch. These are often called dead in shell.

Incubation Tips

- Before you put your eggs into any incubator, make sure it has been sterilised with an incubation disinfectant (or as a minimum warm soap and water if you don't have this). This will kill bacteria that multiply rapidly in the warm temperature of the incubator.
- Plug in your incubator and make sure the temperature is steady at 37.5°C. Always leave it to run overnight to settle before putting eggs in.

- Keep water reservoirs topped up so that adequate humidity can be maintained at all times.
- Candle eggs before putting them into the incubator. Cracked or damaged eggs do not hatch and should be removed after candling

Candling Eggs

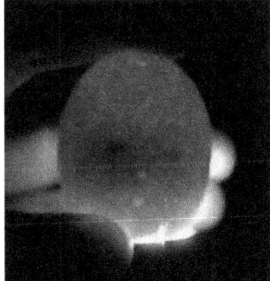

Fertility of eggs cannot be determined before incubating them. It is easiest to see development of the embryo after a week. The most critical period of incubation is the first week so if you do decide to candle your eggs before a week then be very careful with them and do not overheat them.

Eggs with blood rings, cloudy eggs or clear eggs (infertile) should be removed when detected. The photo to the right shows an egg that was candled after 8 days. If you can't see much, do this in the dark. It may also help to tip the egg gently from side to side so you can see the inside of the egg moving and see what are patches on the egg shell and what is inside. The developing spider like veins and a small dark embryo can be seen. If you look carefully and have a bit of luck with the positioning of the embryo, you can often see a small heart beating away. I usually candle after 7 days and again at around 14 days.

The Air Sack

An Air Sack is formed at the broad end of the egg shortly after an egg is laid. There is a membrane between this and where the chick is developing. When candling periodically through the incubation period, this is the best method of judging normal development and you will see this increase in size up until the point that the chick breaks through into this air sack.

The Hatch

*A chick will usually 'pip' the shell a few hours after breaking into the air sack so she can breathe but a full hatch can take 12 or more hours from this point so be patient.

*If humidity has been set too high during the incubation period, the chick may pip the shell underneath the shell and drown in the fluids before he can get his beak out of the shell.

*If the humidity has been too low, the air sack will be too large and the chick will be under-developed and may become stuck to the shell, too weak to break free.

If a chick has pipped but does not make any progress, wait 12 hours, then consider breaking the top part of the shell away (but no more…) Some say do not help weak chicks as you are breeding weakness into your flock but there are many reasons why eggs don't hatch. If it is a humidity problem like this or the line is particularly in-bred (often found with exhibition strains) then a little help can usually be given without detrimental effect.

And finally… Do not remove hatched chicks until they are fully dried out. Chicks do not need to eat for 24 hours. This is why they can be shipped around commercially as 'day old chicks'.

Seasons of Chicken Keeping

Spring: This is the season when egg production should be at its peak. Some hens might go "broody" and want to sit and hatch chicks. They'll stop laying during this period, but start up again once they have hatched and raised their chicks, or you break them of their broodiness. Spring is also the season when most people get started with baby chicks.

Summer: Chickens don't handle heat very well at all, so watching for heat exhaustion, adding electrolytes to the water and providing lots of shade is important. Summer treats that provide lots of hydration are a good idea. Egg production might drop off a bit in extreme heat, but in general this should be a good production season. If you had baby chicks in the spring, now is the time when you'll be introducing them to the rest of your flock or getting them outside for the first time.

Fall: This is molting season. This is the time of year when chickens drops their old feathers and grow in nice, new feathers in preparation for winter. Egg laying will likely drop off a bit as your chickens use all their energy to grow in new feathers. The complete molting process can take weeks or even months, depending on the chicken. Roosters molt too and are generally impotent while molting. A chickens' first molt will be around 18 months old. They won't molt that first fall.

Winter: With new feathers, your chickens will be ready to face their first winter. As mentioned before, chickens don't need heat. Scratch grains fed before bedtime will help to keep your flock warm overnight, as will other warming treats. Your spring chicks will lay well their first winter, but following winters will likely slow way down or more likely stop laying all together. You can add supplemental light to your coop to force your chickens to lay through the winter, but I don't recommend that and instead prefer to give my hens a break and let them start laying again naturally come spring.

CHAPTER 8. HEALTH CARE

Chickens, when well cared for and protected from predators, can live to be 10-12 years old, so be prepared for many years of caring for your hens long after their productive years are over.

However, backyard chickens provide many more "services" than just laying eggs. They also act as insect control, weed control, natural fertilizers and still make great moms to new baby chicks long after they stop laying eggs.

It's not difficult to tell when a hen is sick. She'll be hunched up and miserable-looking. It's unlikely she'll be interested in eating anything, even her favourite treats. Unfortunately, by the time she gets to this stage she'll be very sick indeed. Chickens hide illness well, as weakness invites attacks from the others.

If you spend time with your chickens it becomes easier to recognise the small changes that can indicate a problem brewing. Quick action at this point can prevent or minimise losses.

Daily Checks

Give your chickens a quick once over when you open the hen house in the morning. They should be keen to come out and take their turns at the feeder. As you watch them queuing for breakfast, run through the following checklist:

- Any obvious physical problems: injuries, trailing wings, limping?
- Chickens are attracted to blood, so always remove any bird that is bleeding.
- Attitude: should be bright and alert – are there any signs of bullying or feather-pecking?
- Eating and drinking: is any hen not interested in food, or drinking more than normal?
- Feathers: glossy and unbroken (unless in moult).
- Combs: firm and red (youngsters and moulting birds naturally have paler combs). A purple comb suggests heart or circulatory problems.
- Respiratory problems: any watery eyes, snuffles, or rasping breath?
- Crop (the pouch at the base of the neck where food is stored): should be empty before the bird eats. A bulging crop could indicate a blockage.
- Droppings: a normal dropping is firm, dark brown and white. One in ten is sloppier and foamy.

This may seem a lot to think about first thing in the morning, but it soon becomes habit and only takes a few moments. Take your early cuppa down to the hen house with you.

How To Tell If A Hen Is Sick Or Broody

A hen is sitting in the nest-box looking dazed. She doesn't want to come out for breakfast, certainly isn't alert, her feathers are all puffed up and her comb is pale. She's not scoring well on the checklist, but before you phone the vet make sure she's not just broody.

When approached, a broody hen often squeals or 'growls' angrily. Her breast will feel hot, and she may have pulled out some feathers. Pick her up. She will usually be too preoccupied to peck, but wear gloves if necessary! Place her gently on the ground. After a few seconds, she should come back to life and race to the feeder. She'll carry on as normal for a while, before hurrying back to the nest-box. You almost certainly have a broody hen.

If you pick up a sick hen, she'll either stay where you put her or shuffle off to hide somewhere else.

Closer Inspections: For a full picture you need to get close up and personal with your chickens. Try to do this weekly – it needn't take long, but could save you heartache as well as vet's fees.

First catch your chicken. Never chase chickens – a large landing net is the best way to capture unwilling birds. Otherwise wait until they're roosting.

Now give each hen the following once-over:

Weight: Like baggy clothes, feathers disguise a multitude of sins. If you pick up your hens regularly, you'll get to know whether they are lighter or heavier than usual.

Feel the breastbone: sharpness indicates weight loss. This could be due to worms, illness or maybe bullying. A breastbone hidden under fat suggests your girl needs to lay off the treats. Fat chickens aren't healthy and don't lay eggs.

Injuries or swellings: Look for any minor cuts or lumps.

Eyes, ears, nose and vent: All should be clean with no discharge. Check for clear breathing with no rattling noises.

The crop: A full firm crop in a bird that hasn't eaten recently could be impacted (blocked). This prevents food from passing into the digestive system, so it's serious and needs help from a vet. Bad-smelling breath is a sign of sour crop, a fungal infection which also needs the vet's attention.

Under the feathers: Part the feathers to check for lice and mites. Key areas are around the vent, under the wings and on top of the head (including ear canals). White clumps stuck to feather shafts are lice eggs, while a greasy black mass is northern fowl mite. Treat both flock and housing. (Red mite live in the hen house, rarely on the birds themselves.)

Legs and feet: Raised scales are a sign of scaly leg mite, while a swelling under the foot could be 'bumblefoot,' caused by an infected injury. Both conditions require prompt treatment. If lumps of mud have set like concrete around the feet, don't try to pull them off – soak them with warm, soapy water.

Trim overgrown nails: Now give your feathered friend a small tit-bit as a reward, even if she hasn't been particularly co-operative – with any luck she'll be more obliging next time!

Vaccinating Chickens

Vaccination can be a good way to prevent or reduce the effect of a specific disease in poultry although it is not a substitute for good husbandry. It can be helpful to understand disease classifications to understand what you can protect against by vaccinating chickens: There are Viruses, Mycoplasma, Bacteria, Fungi, Protozoa, and Parasites.

- Viruses can be prevented through cleanliness and vaccination.
- Organisms of all other types of diseases can be killed by chemicals that kill cells, specifically those of micro-organisms.
- Vaccines can be effective in reducing disease in birds, but birds that are exposed to the disease usually still become infected with it and can pass on disease organisms to other birds.

Commercial poultry of course are vaccinated to protect them against a multitude of diseases but commercial operations rarely keep birds past 2 years of age and usually operate an all-in all-out policy to minimise the risk of infection.

As backyard chicken keepers, we often add birds of different ages gradually to our flock. These have different levels of inhereted immunity and older birds could be carriers of diseases. To add to the risk of picking up a disease, some of us buy birds from shows or auctions where many birds have been brought together, increasing the risk of picking up disease. A few of us take birds to shows where they could potentially pick diseases up before bringing them home too.

Vaccination, is not usually an option for small breeders and owners of small flocks since most vaccines come in vials of a minimum of 500 or 1000 doses. Unfortunately, small flocks of birds can suffer from diseases which could be controlled by vaccination.

Most Hybrid chickens come vaccinated. This is because many birds are usually bought and raised at the same time making vaccination more cost effective. Mixing vaccinated and unvaccinated birds isn't recommended, especially when they are young. A common mistake is mixing vaccinated hybrids with unvaccinated pure breeds. Whilst vaccinated birds won't show the clinical signs of a disease like Marek's, they can still carry it and spread it to unvaccinated birds. It is impossible to work out which birds are the disease carrying birds, so you'll go on spreading the virus around the unvaccinated birds in your flock.

Should I vaccinate chickens or not?

Vaccination can only be done at a young age. Most vaccines have to be given during the first few weeks of a chick's life. If you are hatching reasonable numbers of birds, it can be more cost effective, vaccines aren't that expensive unless you've only got a handful of birds to vaccinate.

Deciding whether or not to vaccinate is a difficult choice. What is the likelihood that your birds will be exposed to a disease? How much will it cost to buy the vaccines and equipment with which to administer them (or to ask a vet to do it for you)? If new birds are never introduced and the birds that leave never come back, the chance of picking up a disease is a lot less. You may decide this is the best way to proceed and not to vaccinate.

Some breeds like the Sebright and Silkie are highly susceptible to Marek's disease. One or two suppliers (who keep very large numbers of birds) that I have come across do vaccinate their birds but most, do not.

Personally, I now hatch all of my own eggs to ensure I avoid most diseases, although I do admit to bringing in vaccinated hybrid layers in. These are kept in a different part of the garden so aren't mixing with my pure breeds. If you practice good husbandry and ensure you do not bring new birds in that may also carry disease then you stand a good chance of keeping a healthy flock.

Stress and Chickens

Stress is a major contributor to ill health in chickens and can also make them more prone to a number of vices such as feather picking, egg eating, comb or vent pecking. Chickens kept in intensive conditions are constantly subjected to stress which is why farmers see such high mortality rates and have to pay out to keep birds healthy and make them productive. Fortunately, keeping chickens in our back garden isn't exactly intensive as long as they have a sufficiently large run or are let out of their run regularly to free-range although there are plenty of other times when chickens can suffer from stress.

However, stress is best avoided whenever possible and a little bit of care and forethought can dramatically reduce stress in your birds.

So how do we know what stresses chickens? Well, some years ago, there were studies done that measured the stress hormone 'corticosterone' of birds in different situations and it is this research that has enabled us to understand the stressors.

Stressors: As well as intensive conditions causing stress, the other main stressors can seem quite trivial to us.

Handling: This is one of the biggest stressors. Chickens are a prey species so naturally, if caught and picked up, they become stressed. Whilst regular handling is important for health checks, chasing a bird around a run for 5 minutes every time will not help. Try to catch birds in a confined area such as a house quickly and calmly. Hold the wings firmly and then transfer the bird to the holding position with your right hand underneath her, breast in the palm of your hand, fingers holding the tops of the legs. Her head should be underneath your arm so her head is looking behind you. Use your left hand to examine her.

Introducing new chickens: Chickens are flock animals that have a pecking order. It is thought the ancestors to our chickens, the Red Jungle Fowl of South East Asia use the pecking order to assist in their survival. If every bird has her place, when it comes to feeding time, each one can have her turn and they don't have to spend precious time arguing which may alert predators to their where-abouts. Every hen knows her place in the pecking order and by introducing new birds, the pecking order is upset. No hen knows where she stands and this will cause arguments and considerable stress for days until they have sorted themselves out into a 'new flock'.

Lack of food or water: This stress is completely avoidable of course but we all have those one off days when we suddenly realise that our birds have run out of water for one reason or another. A leaky water container, frozen water or just a forgetful moment!

Extreme heat: Chickens don't sweat. To cool down, a chicken must either take on cool water (and excrete more to lose the excess fluids and some heat) or pant which removes heat through the air they exhale. Chickens are much better equipped to deal with the cold and can keep their body temperature up by eating more and trapping air inside their feathers to insulate themselves thermally. Heat will cause chickens to become stressed.

A new environment: This can be taking a bird to a show, getting your birds for the first time or just moving them to a different house or run. Another environmental change that is hard to avoid but causes considerable stress for your birds is when there has been a covering of snow.

Egg laying: This is surprising since this is a natural things that chickens do but egg laying does cause stress on your hens. Giving them a peaceful, private, darkened nest box can help. Try not to disturb hens that are in the process of laying.

Predation: Foxes or other predators visiting the garden on a regular basis are likely to cause stress. In the extreme case, after a fox attack, even though a chicken may survive the wounds inflicted by a fox (he grabs a mouth full of her feathers for example and the chicken escapes), she can still die because of the stress.

Routine Task

The following routine tasks will give you an idea of what you will need to think about doing at the various times if you keep chickens. These are my routine tasks:

Daily Routine

- Taking water to chickens: Fresh food and water needs to be provided. Pelleted feeds can stay fresh for a week inside a hopper so that they are dispensed ad-lib as the hens require food, however it will soon go mouldy and cause disease if it is not kept dry. Place food containers under cover or purchase a rain hat to keep the rain off. Clean water containers with a small hand brush before refilling them with fresh water.
- A quick 1 minute health check – stop for a minute and observe. Make sure everything appears normal.
- Collect eggs and keep an eye out for broody hens over the spring and summer months.
- Scatter a handful of corn per bird in the late afternoon as a treat.
- Essential: Close the pop hole at night and open it in the morning to protect chickens from predators (especially foxes). Open the coop as soon as you are awake and it is light outside, close it at dusk as soon as your chickens have gone to roost for the night. An automatic doorkeeper has been one of the most useful items I have bought to lock up my chickens at dusk and let them out in the mornings. It is one of the more expensive items I have bought but it is very reliable (the batteries last well over a year) and I am not in a panic trying to get home as it gets dark and the best bit…. I get to have a little extra sleep in on the weekend!

Weekly Routine

- Chicken houses should be cleaned out at least weekly to prevent a build up of organic matter, which puts your birds at more risk from respiratory problems and disease. Between May and October, check perch ends and cracks for Red Mite. They are very common and the sooner you find them, the easier it is to get rid of them.
- Clean feed hoppers – a wipe will sometimes do.
- Provide fresh greens at least twice a week, more often if chickens don't have reasonable free range or if grass is short / there is snow on the ground.
- Check grit hoppers and top up as necessary.
- 5 minute check: Pick up a couple of birds and give them a quick health check. Check that they haven't lost weight and examine between their feathers, particularly around the vent area for lice.
- Check your stocks and re-order as necessary.

Monthly Routine

- Give 2% Apple Cider Vinegar (ACV) in the water for one week a month. I always do this on the first week of every month so that I don't forget.
- Feed Verm-X monthly at 2.5g per bird.

Month Task To Complete

January: Think about breeding. 2 to 3 year old chickens are best for breeding as they have resistance to disease and their eggs are now a good size. Get incubators tested and ready for use if you plan on hatching this spring. Add a vitamin supplement to the water if the weather is cold and rub Vassalene into large combed cockerels such as Leghorns to protect against hard frosts. Provide regular greens when the ground is frozen. If snow falls, clear the ground immediately in front of their house so they can get out.

February: Order spare heat lamps for brooders, chick crumbs and anything else required if you are going to incubate. Add a vitamin supplement to the water to birds that are breeding or if the weather is cold. Continue rubbing vaseline onto the combs of large combed cockerels if necessary. Provide regular greens when the ground is frozen. Check fertility of eggs in incubator.

March: Collect eggs and start incubating to get new stock. Fertility should now be at its best and all hens should be laying by now. Add gravel, sand or wood chippings to well used ground as it turns to mud in the rain. Worm the flock with Flubenvet.

April: Spring clean chicken houses. Set broody hens and tend to chicks if you have hatched them. If you have a cockerel, fit poultry saddles to hens so they don't lose feathers from their backs. Build or buy any new housing required for new birds. Remember not to mix young chicks / growers with older birds but let them out on warmer days for a couple of hours around mid-day to get some fresh grass.

May: Red mite season begins – start preventative red mite treatment. Let chicks / growers out onto grass in covered runs and make sure they are locked up at night.

June: Continue preventative red mite treatment. Inspect fencing fully as June to September is a popular time for fox attacks. Make sure birds have shade and their water is not in the sunlight so they can cool themselves off by drinking.

July: Continue preventative red mite treatment. Get any painting or treating of houses done when the sun is shining. As chicks can be sexed, remove unwanted cockerels as they will cost you to keep and won't be productive.

August: Continue preventative red mite treatment. As chickens come into moult, give them extra vitamins, a handful of dried catfood (for extra protein) and ACV to help them to grow new feathers.

September: Continue preventative red mite treatment. Move this years hatch (now pullets) to their new accommodation or integrate them with the flock as they will soon start to lay. Worm the flock. Repair houses and runs that need fixing before the winter. Replace sand or chippings if used in smaller runs.

October: Red Mite Season Ends – Stop preventative red mite treatment as weather turns cold. Review stock levels: Don't over-winter stock that isn't going to be of use next year. Remember young cockerels who get on fine now will become competitive and start to fight in the breeding season.

November: Make sure you have sufficient water containers for the freezing weather to come. Consider visiting some of the poultry shows that are held during the Autumn. Make sure hen houses are draft proof.

December: Add a vitamin supplement to the water every other week if the weather is cold. Provide regular greens when the ground is frozen and extra corn so they have more fat (from the maize) to produce more heat. Ensure hens can get shelter when the weather is bad, especially in cold winds and rain.

What to Keep in Stock

I have compiled these lists based on what I keep in stock for my 20 chickens. I have first listed what I would consider essential to looking after your hens and the second list is what I consider useful to have in stock just in case. I have not included common items such as food, grit or bedding and cleaning equipment. The products can of course vary slightly depending on your preferences or local supplier availability. I haven't included food or mixed corn.

My Essential 'Must Have' list (in no particular order):

- **Apple Cider Vinegar or ACV:** It's given to my girls for one week monthly. The product you buy must be unrefined to get the benefit and usually is cloudy. Don't buy human grade ACV which is filtered and not as beneficial. I mix it at 2% dilution rate. It has anti-bacterial benefits and discourages coccisidiosis and worms by making the gut slightly acidic.
- **Poultry Shield:** It is a very safe detergent that is good for removing organic matter and killing bacteria that cause diseases. It does not contain any poisons or caustic chemicals like some household products. It is very good for controlling Red Mite by washing off their waxy outer coating. Poultry Shield gets into cracks where mites hide and where powders can't reach.
- **Diatom:** A wonderful product that I would not be without. Totally organic (made of fossilised diatoms). I use this in feed to help keep worms at bay (5% in feed from time to time) and also dust in the coop during the summer months for Red Mite control.

- **Red Mite Powder:** It's suitable for organic production and can be used on the hens themselves. Mites are usually in the house, only going onto birds at night for a feed so this helps protect them at night. You can also use Red Mite Powder around the nest boxes. It contains tea tree and always leaves the nest boxes smelling wonderful.
- **Battles Poultry Drink:** I use this multi-vitamin drink at times of stress and during the moult. It is particularly good if birds are recovering from Red Mite since it contains iron phosphorus potassium manganese and copper. It contains a selection of 5 minerals in a high energy sugar syrup base. And supports all round condition and health. Just add directly to the drinking water or the daily ration.

My 'Useful to Have' list (in no particular order):

- **Cod Liver Oil:** A small amount of cod liver oil added to feed during the moult, helps birds to re-grow feathers. It's also useful for mixing wormer with feeds – A small amount in a pot mixed with a wormer helps to get the powder to stick to the pellets without going to the bottom of the hopper.
- Verm-X: It's a herbal supplement that helps prevent internal parasites (worms) and keeps birds in good condition. I use Verm-X regularly but use Flubenvet if I have a confirmed case of worms (I test with a worm count kit above first and 99% of the time have the all-clear). It is easy to administer with the 3.5g scoop that comes in the pot. The recommended dose is one scoop per bird per day.
- **Dummy Eggs:** I use dummy (or pot) eggs when I have a broody hen and I want her to sit for a few days to make sure she is keen. Once she's keen, she can be transferred to a broody coop and can sit on some eggs.
- **Spare Water Container:** If one of my water containers freezes or gets broken by accident, I always keep a spare. A 6 litre container lasts my 20 girls 2 days, (although ideally you should be giving your hens fresh water daily) but sometimes I will empty some out on the second day to freshen it up and I still have a little spare in the container. 4 litres should be enough for 12 hens.

CHAPTER 9. PEST MANAGEMENT AND MAINTENANCE

You can significantly eliminate potential problems in your chicken coop by simply keeping the area clean and performing regular maintenance duties

Red Mite

I would rate red mites as being one of the biggest problems you will face when keeping chickens. Red Mites live in the cracks of chicken houses (typically under perch ends) coming out at night, crawling onto your birds for a feed. They start off as very small greyish-white mites that swell up into red coloured mites after a feed and at their biggest are only 1mm so small numbers of them can be hard to spot unless you know what to look for.

You will often find a grey ash like deposit around perch ends which is where the mites have been and if you lift the perch, you will see clumps of mites. Red Mite in chickens' houses are active during the warmer months, usually May to October and will become dormant over the winter. They multiply at an incredible rate: their life cycle is just 7-10 days. In other words from hatching from an egg to being an adult laying hundreds of eggs takes just a week if conditions are right.

Be Proactive

The best course of action is to check for red mite routinely when you clean your chicken house out and use some preventative treatment to the house before they get a hold. You will get to know the places to look and once you have found small numbers of them, you can treat the house to keep numbers under control.

Are there Red Mite in your Chicken House?

People normally discover Red Mite when they are over-run by them. When hens are being bitten, they can refuse to go in to roost at night, they will become anaemic and their combs will go pale. They will often stop laying and you may find red blood stains on eggs (squashed Red Mites). Eventually, you will start to see losses in the flock.

Checking for Red Mite in Chickens Houses

Red Mite will hide away in the daytime but can often be seen if you lift perches, examining the ends. They will usually come swarming out if you treat the cracks with Poultry Shield but by far the easiest way to check to see if there are red mite is to take a piece of white kitchen roll and to rub it along the underside of the perch when your hens are roosting (in the dark).

Look at the tissue and if there are Red Mite heading back from their feed, they will be squashed on the kitchen roll as streaks of blood.

Getting Rid of Red Mite

It is very hard to get rid of them completely so it is often better to get the numbers down and then find a way of keeping them down that doesn't involve you spending hours on cleaning the house out. There are lots of different treatments that people use, some more effective than others but I will focus on what I do and have found to be the most successful for me.

If you haven't got red mite and the weather is warm enough for them then skip step 1 and go straight to step 2. Preventative Measures.

1. Getting rid of an infestation: If you find lots of red mite in the coop, it's time for a big clean up that will take a couple of hours initially, then an hour every 5 to 7 days for at least 2 more weeks.

The products I have found to work the best (that are relatively safe) are Poultry Shield and Diatom. These two are not 'knock down' products as such, they do take a little while to work but are none the less very effective. I also use Red Mite Powder on the hens themselves to help them through the night when the Mites are active.

Here is what I do with the Poultry Shield...

- Remove all birds from the house.
- Strip the house down as much as possible.
- Clean the house out – be careful where the bedding is going as red mite live for 6 months without a feed and will find a new home If they can. Ideally seal the bedding in bin bags or burn.
- Mix up as many watering cans of poultry shield mixture as is needed, as per the instructions on the label.
- 'Water' all cracks in the chicken house, concentrating where there are perch ends and concentrations of red mite.
- Leave to soak for 15 minutes
- Red mites will be coming out. Cover them and the cracks with poultry shield again.
- Wait 15 minutes
- Hose out the house, concentrating on getting the pressure jet into the cracks and so on.
- Leave the house to dry.

Poultry Shield is a mild detergent and 'washes' the waxy coat off the red mites. It is also good for removing organic matter from the hen house so is useful for cleaning. I wouldn't be without this.

After using the Poultry Shield, when the house is dry, I use Diatom. Diatom is made of micro skeletons of fossilised remains of diatoms. These were once a kind of algae found in water. They are microscopically sharp and pierce the outer waxy coating of the mites which causes them to dry out and die. The second step also double up as my 'preventative' measures if you haven't yet got a bad infestation

2. Preventative Measures: Dust the ends of the perches / nest boxes and where ever else you found concentrations of red mites when cleaning. Rub as much into the perches as you can. Red mite will avoid the diatom and will crawl around it if they can, so make sure they have to crawl through it to get a feed.

Repeat every couple of days for as long as you see signs of red mite in the coop. Repeat the whole cleaning process if there are still lots of mites in 5 to 7 days. You will find you might not need to spend as long on the washing as there won't be as many mites.

Very Important: Make sure you repeat it before 7 days so that the mites don't have a chance to lay more eggs. A few mites become a lot in a very short space of time.

If you have a felt roof on your chicken house and they get underneath, it is usually impossible to get rid of them without removing the felt, cleaning and re-felting.

Finally, I will dust the hens down between their feathers with Red Mite Powder to give them some respite during the night when the mites are active.

Protecting Your Chicken

Predators

Keeping chickens safe from predators has to be top on your list of priorities. There are several animals around the World that will prey on chickens and it's your job to keep them safe and not letting them become part of the local wildlife's food chain.

Foxes: The number one predator for chickens is of course the fox but did you know that some people also have badgers killing their chickens? Most inexperienced people will think a fox has visited however this isn't always the case.

Badgers: Badgers are incredibly strong and if they are hungry, they have been known to tear off wooden panels of chicken houses that aren't secure and tear open pop holes to get to chickens. They will usually kill and take one bird but might come back for a second. They usually work alone.

Domestic Cats: Cats aren't generally a problem to fully grown chickens and mine have never bothered with young 'growers'. They seem more interested in chicks though and shouldn't be trusted. Some people have had problems, usually with a specific cat in the neighbourhood and with smaller bantam chickens. It's very difficult to keep cats out completely.

Rats and Mice: Pests such as rats and mice can be a problem as they spread diseases, eat valuable feed supplies and (rats) can steal eggs and gnaw at doors, wires and even chickens feet. Usually only one or the other are present and rats can be quite discreet so if there are no mice then be suspicious of rats

www.ingramcontent.com/pod-product-compliance
Lightning Source LLC
LaVergne TN
LVHW081525060526
838200LV00044B/2002